Password Book
Belongs to:

_____

Website_____

Username_____

Password_____

Info/Notes_____

_____

_____

_____

Website_____

Username_____

Password_____

Info/Notes_____

_____

_____

_____

Website_____

Username_____

Password_____

Info/Notes_____

_____

_____

_____

Website_____
Username_____
Password_____
Info/Notes_____
_____
_____
_____
_____

Website_____
Username_____
Password_____
Info/Notes_____
_____
_____
_____
_____

Website_____
Username_____
Password_____
Info/Notes_____
_____
_____
_____

Website_____
Username_____
Password_____
Info/Notes_____
_____
_____
_____

Website_____
Username_____
Password_____
Info/Notes_____
_____
_____
_____

Website_____
Username_____
Password_____
Info/Notes_____
_____
_____
_____

Website_____

Username_____

Password_____

Info/Notes_____

_____

_____

_____

Website_____

Username_____

Password_____

Info/Notes_____

_____

_____

_____

Website_____

Username_____

Password_____

Info/Notes_____

_____

_____

_____

Website_____

Username_____

Password_____

Info/Notes_____

_____

_____

_____

Website_____

Username_____

Password_____

Info/Notes_____

_____

_____

_____

Website_____

Username_____

Password_____

Info/Notes_____

_____

_____

_____

Website_____
Username_____
Password_____
Info/Notes_____
_____
_____
_____

Website_____
Username_____
Password_____
Info/Notes_____
_____
_____
_____

Website_____
Username_____
Password_____
Info/Notes_____
_____
_____
_____

Website_____
Username_____
Password_____
Info/Notes_____

_____
_____
_____

Website_____
Username_____
Password_____
Info/Notes_____

_____
_____
_____

Website_____
Username_____
Password_____
Info/Notes_____

_____
_____
_____

Website_____
Username_____
Password_____
Info/Notes_____
_____
_____
_____

Website_____
Username_____
Password_____
Info/Notes_____
_____
_____
_____

Website_____
Username_____
Password_____
Info/Notes_____
_____
_____
_____

Website_____
Username_____
Password_____
Info/Notes_____

_____
_____
_____

Website_____
Username_____
Password_____
Info/Notes_____

_____
_____
_____

Website_____
Username_____
Password_____
Info/Notes_____

_____
_____
_____

Website_____
Username_____
Password_____
Info/Notes_____
_____
_____
_____
_____

Website_____
Username_____
Password_____
Info/Notes_____
_____
_____
_____

Website_____
Username_____
Password_____
Info/Notes_____
_____
_____
_____

Website_____
Username_____
Password_____
Info/Notes_____

_____
_____
_____

Website_____
Username_____
Password_____
Info/Notes_____

_____
_____
_____

Website_____
Username_____
Password_____
Info/Notes_____

_____
_____
_____

Website_____
Username_____
Password_____
Info/Notes_____
_____
_____
_____
_____

Website_____
Username_____
Password_____
Info/Notes_____
_____
_____
_____
_____

Website_____
Username_____
Password_____
Info/Notes_____
_____
_____
_____

Website_____
Username_____
Password_____
Info/Notes_____

_____
_____
_____

Website_____
Username_____
Password_____
Info/Notes_____

_____
_____
_____

Website_____
Username_____
Password_____
Info/Notes_____

_____
_____
_____

Website_____
Username_____
Password_____
Info/Notes_____
_____
_____
_____
_____

Website_____
Username_____
Password_____
Info/Notes_____
_____
_____
_____

Website_____
Username_____
Password_____
Info/Notes_____
_____
_____
_____

Website_____
Username_____
Password_____
Info/Notes_____
_____
_____
_____

Website_____
Username_____
Password_____
Info/Notes_____
_____
_____
_____

Website_____
Username_____
Password_____
Info/Notes_____
_____
_____
_____

Website_____
Username_____
Password_____
Info/Notes_____

_____
_____
_____

Website_____
Username_____
Password_____
Info/Notes_____

_____
_____
_____

Website_____
Username_____
Password_____
Info/Notes_____

_____
_____
_____

Website_____

Username_____

Password_____

Info/Notes_____

_____

_____

_____

Website_____

Username_____

Password_____

Info/Notes_____

_____

_____

_____

Website_____

Username_____

Password_____

Info/Notes_____

_____

_____

_____

Website_____
Username_____
Password_____
Info/Notes_____

_____
_____
_____

Website_____
Username_____
Password_____
Info/Notes_____

_____
_____
_____

Website_____
Username_____
Password_____
Info/Notes_____

_____
_____
_____

Website_____
Username_____
Password_____
Info/Notes_____

_____
_____
_____

Website_____
Username_____
Password_____
Info/Notes_____

_____
_____
_____

Website_____
Username_____
Password_____
Info/Notes_____

_____
_____
_____

Website_____
Username_____
Password_____
Info/Notes_____
_____
_____
_____
_____

Website_____
Username_____
Password_____
Info/Notes_____
_____
_____
_____
_____

Website_____
Username_____
Password_____
Info/Notes_____
_____
_____
_____

Website_____
Username_____
Password_____
Info/Notes_____
_____
_____
_____

Website_____
Username_____
Password_____
Info/Notes_____
_____
_____
_____

Website_____
Username_____
Password_____
Info/Notes_____
_____
_____
_____

Website_____
Username_____
Password_____
Info/Notes_____
_____
_____
_____

Website_____
Username_____
Password_____
Info/Notes_____
_____
_____
_____

Website_____
Username_____
Password_____
Info/Notes_____
_____
_____
_____

Website_____

Username_____

Password_____

Info/Notes_____

_____

_____

_____

Website_____

Username_____

Password_____

Info/Notes_____

_____

_____

_____

Website_____

Username_____

Password_____

Info/Notes_____

_____

_____

_____

Website_____
Username_____
Password_____
Info/Notes_____
_____
_____
_____
_____

Website_____
Username_____
Password_____
Info/Notes_____
_____
_____
_____
_____

Website_____
Username_____
Password_____
Info/Notes_____
_____
_____
_____

Website_____
Username_____
Password_____
Info/Notes_____

_____
_____
_____

Website_____
Username_____
Password_____
Info/Notes_____

_____
_____
_____

Website_____
Username_____
Password_____
Info/Notes_____

_____
_____
_____

Website_____
Username_____
Password_____
Info/Notes_____
_____
_____
_____
_____

Website_____
Username_____
Password_____
Info/Notes_____
_____
_____
_____
_____

Website_____
Username_____
Password_____
Info/Notes_____
_____
_____
_____

Website_____

Username_____

Password_____

Info/Notes_____

_____

_____

_____

Website_____

Username_____

Password_____

Info/Notes_____

_____

_____

_____

Website_____

Username_____

Password_____

Info/Notes_____

_____

_____

_____

Website_____
Username_____
Password_____
Info/Notes_____
_____
_____
_____
_____

Website_____
Username_____
Password_____
Info/Notes_____
_____
_____
_____
_____

Website_____
Username_____
Password_____
Info/Notes_____
_____
_____
_____

Website_____
Username_____
Password_____
Info/Notes_____

_____
_____
_____

Website_____
Username_____
Password_____
Info/Notes_____

_____
_____
_____

Website_____
Username_____
Password_____
Info/Notes_____

_____
_____
_____

Website_____
Username_____
Password_____
Info/Notes_____

_____
_____
_____
_____

Website_____
Username_____
Password_____
Info/Notes_____

_____
_____
_____
_____

Website_____
Username_____
Password_____
Info/Notes_____

_____
_____
_____

Website_____

Username_____

Password_____

Info/Notes_____

_____

_____

_____

Website_____

Username_____

Password_____

Info/Notes_____

_____

_____

_____

Website_____

Username_____

Password_____

Info/Notes_____

_____

_____

_____

Website_____
Username_____
Password_____
Info/Notes_____
_____
_____
_____
_____

Website_____
Username_____
Password_____
Info/Notes_____
_____
_____
_____
_____

Website_____
Username_____
Password_____
Info/Notes_____
_____
_____
_____

Website_____
Username_____
Password_____
Info/Notes_____
_____
_____
_____
_____

Website_____
Username_____
Password_____
Info/Notes_____
_____
_____
_____
_____

Website_____
Username_____
Password_____
Info/Notes_____
_____
_____
_____

Website_____
Username_____
Password_____
Info/Notes_____
_____
_____
_____
_____

Website_____
Username_____
Password_____
Info/Notes_____
_____
_____
_____
_____

Website_____
Username_____
Password_____
Info/Notes_____
_____
_____
_____

Website_____
Username_____
Password_____
Info/Notes_____

_____
_____
_____

Website_____
Username_____
Password_____
Info/Notes_____

_____
_____
_____

Website_____
Username_____
Password_____
Info/Notes_____

_____
_____
_____

Website_____
Username_____
Password_____
Info/Notes_____
_____
_____
_____
_____

Website_____
Username_____
Password_____
Info/Notes_____
_____
_____
_____
_____

Website_____
Username_____
Password_____
Info/Notes_____
_____
_____
_____

Website_____

Username_____

Password_____

Info/Notes_____

_____

_____

_____

Website_____

Username_____

Password_____

Info/Notes_____

_____

_____

_____

Website_____

Username_____

Password_____

Info/Notes_____

_____

_____

_____

Website_____
Username_____
Password_____
Info/Notes_____

_____
_____
_____
_____

Website_____
Username_____
Password_____
Info/Notes_____

_____
_____
_____

Website_____
Username_____
Password_____
Info/Notes_____

_____
_____
_____

Website_____

Username_____

Password_____

Info/Notes_____

_____

_____

_____

_____

Website_____

Username_____

Password_____

Info/Notes_____

_____

_____

_____

_____

Website_____

Username_____

Password_____

Info/Notes_____

_____

_____

_____

Website_____

Username_____

Password_____

Info/Notes_____

_____

_____

_____

Website_____

Username_____

Password_____

Info/Notes_____

_____

_____

_____

Website_____

Username_____

Password_____

Info/Notes_____

_____

_____

_____

Website_____
Username_____
Password_____
Info/Notes_____
_____
_____
_____

Website_____
Username_____
Password_____
Info/Notes_____
_____
_____
_____

Website_____
Username_____
Password_____
Info/Notes_____
_____
_____
_____

Website_____
Username_____
Password_____
Info/Notes_____
_____
_____
_____

Website_____
Username_____
Password_____
Info/Notes_____
_____
_____
_____

Website_____
Username_____
Password_____
Info/Notes_____
_____
_____
_____

Website_____

Username_____

Password_____

Info/Notes_____

_____

_____

_____

Website_____

Username_____

Password_____

Info/Notes_____

_____

_____

_____

Website_____

Username_____

Password_____

Info/Notes_____

_____

_____

_____

Website_____
Username_____
Password_____
Info/Notes_____
_____
_____
_____
_____

Website_____
Username_____
Password_____
Info/Notes_____
_____
_____
_____
_____

Website_____
Username_____
Password_____
Info/Notes_____
_____
_____
_____

Website_____
Username_____
Password_____
Info/Notes_____
_____
_____
_____

Website_____
Username_____
Password_____
Info/Notes_____
_____
_____
_____

Website_____
Username_____
Password_____
Info/Notes_____
_____
_____
_____

Website_____
Username_____
Password_____
Info/Notes_____
_____
_____
_____

Website_____
Username_____
Password_____
Info/Notes_____
_____
_____
_____

Website_____
Username_____
Password_____
Info/Notes_____
_____
_____
_____

Website_____
Username_____
Password_____
Info/Notes_____

_____
_____
_____

Website_____
Username_____
Password_____
Info/Notes_____

_____
_____
_____

Website_____
Username_____
Password_____
Info/Notes_____

_____
_____
_____

Website_____
Username_____
Password_____
Info/Notes_____
_____
_____
_____

Website_____
Username_____
Password_____
Info/Notes_____
_____
_____
_____

Website_____
Username_____
Password_____
Info/Notes_____
_____
_____
_____

Website_____
Username_____
Password_____
Info/Notes_____
_____
_____
_____

Website_____
Username_____
Password_____
Info/Notes_____
_____
_____
_____

Website_____
Username_____
Password_____
Info/Notes_____
_____
_____
_____

Website_____
Username_____
Password_____
Info/Notes_____
_____
_____
_____
_____

Website_____
Username_____
Password_____
Info/Notes_____
_____
_____
_____
_____

Website_____
Username_____
Password_____
Info/Notes_____
_____
_____
_____

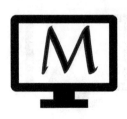

Website_____
Username_____
Password_____
Info/Notes_____

_____

_____

_____

_____

Website_____
Username_____
Password_____
Info/Notes_____

_____

_____

_____

Website_____
Username_____
Password_____
Info/Notes_____

_____

_____

_____

Website_____
Username_____
Password_____
Info/Notes_____
_____
_____
_____

Website_____
Username_____
Password_____
Info/Notes_____
_____
_____
_____

Website_____
Username_____
Password_____
Info/Notes_____
_____
_____
_____

Website_____
Username_____
Password_____
Info/Notes_____

_____
_____
_____

Website_____
Username_____
Password_____
Info/Notes_____

_____
_____
_____

Website_____
Username_____
Password_____
Info/Notes_____

_____
_____
_____

Website_____
Username_____
Password_____
Info/Notes_____
_____
_____
_____
_____

Website_____
Username_____
Password_____
Info/Notes_____
_____
_____
_____
_____

Website_____
Username_____
Password_____
Info/Notes_____
_____
_____
_____

Website_____
Username_____
Password_____
Info/Notes_____

_____
_____
_____

Website_____
Username_____
Password_____
Info/Notes_____

_____
_____
_____

Website_____
Username_____
Password_____
Info/Notes_____

_____
_____
_____

Website_____
Username_____
Password_____
Info/Notes_____

_____
_____
_____

Website_____
Username_____
Password_____
Info/Notes_____

_____
_____
_____

Website_____
Username_____
Password_____
Info/Notes_____

_____
_____
_____

Website_____
Username_____
Password_____
Info/Notes_____
_____
_____
_____

Website_____
Username_____
Password_____
Info/Notes_____
_____
_____
_____

Website_____
Username_____
Password_____
Info/Notes_____
_____
_____
_____

Website_____
Username_____
Password_____
Info/Notes_____

_____
_____
_____
_____

Website_____
Username_____
Password_____
Info/Notes_____

_____
_____
_____
_____

Website_____
Username_____
Password_____
Info/Notes_____

_____
_____
_____

Website_____
Username_____
Password_____
Info/Notes_____

_____
_____
_____

Website_____
Username_____
Password_____
Info/Notes_____

_____
_____
_____

Website_____
Username_____
Password_____
Info/Notes_____

_____
_____
_____

Website_____
Username_____
Password_____
Info/Notes_____

_____
_____
_____
_____

Website_____
Username_____
Password_____
Info/Notes_____

_____
_____
_____

Website_____
Username_____
Password_____
Info/Notes_____

_____
_____
_____

Website_____
Username_____
Password_____
Info/Notes_____
_____
_____
_____

Website_____
Username_____
Password_____
Info/Notes_____
_____
_____
_____

Website_____
Username_____
Password_____
Info/Notes_____
_____
_____
_____

Website_____

Username_____

Password_____

Info/Notes_____

_____

_____

_____

_____

Website_____

Username_____

Password_____

Info/Notes_____

_____

_____

_____

_____

Website_____

Username_____

Password_____

Info/Notes_____

_____

_____

_____

Website_____
Username_____
Password_____
Info/Notes_____

_____
_____
_____

Website_____
Username_____
Password_____
Info/Notes_____

_____
_____
_____

Website_____
Username_____
Password_____
Info/Notes_____

_____
_____
_____

Website_____
Username_____
Password_____
Info/Notes_____

_____
_____
_____
_____

Website_____
Username_____
Password_____
Info/Notes_____

_____
_____
_____

Website_____
Username_____
Password_____
Info/Notes_____

_____
_____
_____

Website_____
Username_____
Password_____
Info/Notes_____
_____
_____
_____

Website_____
Username_____
Password_____
Info/Notes_____
_____
_____
_____

Website_____
Username_____
Password_____
Info/Notes_____
_____
_____
_____

Website_____
Username_____
Password_____
Info/Notes_____
_____
_____
_____
_____

Website_____
Username_____
Password_____
Info/Notes_____
_____
_____
_____
_____

Website_____
Username_____
Password_____
Info/Notes_____
_____
_____
_____

Website_____
Username_____
Password_____
Info/Notes_____

_____

_____

_____

Website_____
Username_____
Password_____
Info/Notes_____

_____

_____

_____

Website_____
Username_____
Password_____
Info/Notes_____

_____

_____

_____

Website_____
Username_____
Password_____
Info/Notes_____
_____
_____
_____

Website_____
Username_____
Password_____
Info/Notes_____
_____
_____
_____

Website_____
Username_____
Password_____
Info/Notes_____
_____
_____
_____

Website_____
Username_____
Password_____
Info/Notes_____

_____

_____

_____

Website_____
Username_____
Password_____
Info/Notes_____

_____

_____

_____

Website_____
Username_____
Password_____
Info/Notes_____

_____

_____

_____

Website_____
Username_____
Password_____
Info/Notes_____

_____
_____
_____
_____

Website_____
Username_____
Password_____
Info/Notes_____

_____
_____
_____

Website_____
Username_____
Password_____
Info/Notes_____

_____
_____
_____

Website_____
Username_____
Password_____
Info/Notes_____

_____
_____
_____

Website_____
Username_____
Password_____
Info/Notes_____

_____
_____
_____

Website_____
Username_____
Password_____
Info/Notes_____

_____
_____
_____

Website_____

Username_____

Password_____

Info/Notes_____

_____

_____

_____

Website_____

Username_____

Password_____

Info/Notes_____

_____

_____

_____

Website_____

Username_____

Password_____

Info/Notes_____

_____

_____

_____

Website_____
Username_____
Password_____
Info/Notes_____
_____
_____
_____
_____

Website_____
Username_____
Password_____
Info/Notes_____
_____
_____
_____
_____

Website_____
Username_____
Password_____
Info/Notes_____
_____
_____
_____

Website_____
Username_____
Password_____
Info/Notes_____
_____
_____
_____
_____

Website_____
Username_____
Password_____
Info/Notes_____
_____
_____
_____

Website_____
Username_____
Password_____
Info/Notes_____
_____
_____
_____

Website_____

Username_____

Password_____

Info/Notes_____

_____

_____

_____

Website_____

Username_____

Password_____

Info/Notes_____

_____

_____

_____

Website_____

Username_____

Password_____

Info/Notes_____

_____

_____

_____

Website_____
Username_____
Password_____
Info/Notes_____

_____
_____
_____
_____

Website_____
Username_____
Password_____
Info/Notes_____

_____
_____
_____
_____

Website_____
Username_____
Password_____
Info/Notes_____

_____
_____
_____
_____

Website_____
Username_____
Password_____
Info/Notes_____

_____
_____
_____
_____

Website_____
Username_____
Password_____
Info/Notes_____

_____
_____
_____

Website_____
Username_____
Password_____
Info/Notes_____

_____
_____
_____

Website_____
Username_____
Password_____
Info/Notes_____
_____
_____
_____
_____

Website_____
Username_____
Password_____
Info/Notes_____
_____
_____
_____
_____

Website_____
Username_____
Password_____
Info/Notes_____
_____
_____
_____

Website_____
Username_____
Password_____
Info/Notes_____

_____
_____
_____

Website_____
Username_____
Password_____
Info/Notes_____

_____
_____
_____

Website_____
Username_____
Password_____
Info/Notes_____

_____
_____
_____

Website_____

Username_____

Password_____

Info/Notes_____

_____

_____

_____

_____

Website_____

Username_____

Password_____

Info/Notes_____

_____

_____

_____

Website_____

Username_____

Password_____

Info/Notes_____

_____

_____

_____

Website_____
Username_____
Password_____
Info/Notes_____
_____
_____
_____

Website_____
Username_____
Password_____
Info/Notes_____
_____
_____
_____

Website_____
Username_____
Password_____
Info/Notes_____
_____
_____
_____

Website_____
Username_____
Password_____
Info/Notes_____
_____
_____
_____

Website_____
Username_____
Password_____
Info/Notes_____
_____
_____
_____

Website_____
Username_____
Password_____
Info/Notes_____
_____
_____
_____

Website_____
Username_____
Password_____
Info/Notes_____

_____

_____

_____

Website_____
Username_____
Password_____
Info/Notes_____

_____

_____

_____

Website_____
Username_____
Password_____
Info/Notes_____

_____

_____

_____

Website_____
Username_____
Password_____
Info/Notes_____
_____
_____
_____
_____

Website_____
Username_____
Password_____
Info/Notes_____
_____
_____
_____
_____

Website_____
Username_____
Password_____
Info/Notes_____
_____
_____
_____
_____

Website_____
Username_____
Password_____
Info/Notes_____

_____
_____
_____
_____

Website_____
Username_____
Password_____
Info/Notes_____

_____
_____
_____
_____

Website_____
Username_____
Password_____
Info/Notes_____

_____
_____
_____

Website_____
Username_____
Password_____
Info/Notes_____

_____
_____
_____
_____

Website_____
Username_____
Password_____
Info/Notes_____

_____
_____
_____

Website_____
Username_____
Password_____
Info/Notes_____

_____
_____
_____

Website_____
Username_____
Password_____
Info/Notes_____

_____
_____
_____

Website_____
Username_____
Password_____
Info/Notes_____

_____
_____
_____

Website_____
Username_____
Password_____
Info/Notes_____

_____
_____
_____

Website_____
Username_____
Password_____
Info/Notes_____
_____
_____
_____
_____

Website_____
Username_____
Password_____
Info/Notes_____
_____
_____
_____

Website_____
Username_____
Password_____
Info/Notes_____
_____
_____
_____

Website_____
Username_____
Password_____
Info/Notes_____
_____
_____
_____
_____

Website_____
Username_____
Password_____
Info/Notes_____
_____
_____
_____
_____

Website_____
Username_____
Password_____
Info/Notes_____
_____
_____
_____

Website_____
Username_____
Password_____
Info/Notes_____

_____
_____
_____
_____

Website_____
Username_____
Password_____
Info/Notes_____

_____
_____
_____
_____

Website_____
Username_____
Password_____
Info/Notes_____

_____
_____
_____
_____

Website_____
Username_____
Password_____
Info/Notes_____

_____
_____
_____

Website_____
Username_____
Password_____
Info/Notes_____

_____
_____
_____

Website_____
Username_____
Password_____
Info/Notes_____

_____
_____
_____

Website_____
Username_____
Password_____
Info/Notes_____
_____
_____
_____
_____

Website_____
Username_____
Password_____
Info/Notes_____
_____
_____
_____

Website_____
Username_____
Password_____
Info/Notes_____
_____
_____
_____

Website_____
Username_____
Password_____
Info/Notes_____

_____
_____
_____
_____

Website_____
Username_____
Password_____
Info/Notes_____

_____
_____
_____
_____

Website_____
Username_____
Password_____
Info/Notes_____

_____
_____
_____

Website_____
Username_____
Password_____
Info/Notes_____

_____
_____
_____
_____

Website_____
Username_____
Password_____
Info/Notes_____

_____
_____
_____
_____

Website_____
Username_____
Password_____
Info/Notes_____

_____
_____
_____

Website_____
Username_____
Password_____
Info/Notes_____
_____
_____
_____

Website_____
Username_____
Password_____
Info/Notes_____
_____
_____
_____

Website_____
Username_____
Password_____
Info/Notes_____
_____
_____
_____

Website_____
Username_____
Password_____
Info/Notes_____
_____
_____
_____
_____

Website_____
Username_____
Password_____
Info/Notes_____
_____
_____
_____

Website_____
Username_____
Password_____
Info/Notes_____
_____
_____
_____

Website_____
Username_____
Password_____
Info/Notes_____
_____
_____
_____
_____

Website_____
Username_____
Password_____
Info/Notes_____
_____
_____
_____

Website_____
Username_____
Password_____
Info/Notes_____
_____
_____
_____

Website_____
Username_____
Password_____
Info/Notes_____
_____
_____
_____
_____

Website_____
Username_____
Password_____
Info/Notes_____
_____
_____
_____

Website_____
Username_____
Password_____
Info/Notes_____
_____
_____
_____

Website_____

Username_____

Password_____

Info/Notes_____

_____

_____

_____

_____

Website_____

Username_____

Password_____

Info/Notes_____

_____

_____

_____

_____

Website_____

Username_____

Password_____

Info/Notes_____

_____

_____

_____

_____

Website_____
Username_____
Password_____
Info/Notes_____

_____
_____
_____
_____

Website_____
Username_____
Password_____
Info/Notes_____

_____
_____
_____

Website_____
Username_____
Password_____
Info/Notes_____

_____
_____
_____

Website_____
Username_____
Password_____
Info/Notes_____
_____
_____
_____
_____

Website_____
Username_____
Password_____
Info/Notes_____
_____
_____
_____
_____

Website_____
Username_____
Password_____
Info/Notes_____
_____
_____
_____

Website_____
Username_____
Password_____
Info/Notes_____
_____
_____
_____
_____

Website_____
Username_____
Password_____
Info/Notes_____
_____
_____
_____
_____

Website_____
Username_____
Password_____
Info/Notes_____
_____
_____
_____

Website_____
Username_____
Password_____
Info/Notes_____
_____
_____
_____
_____

Website_____
Username_____
Password_____
Info/Notes_____
_____
_____
_____
_____

Website_____
Username_____
Password_____
Info/Notes_____
_____
_____
_____

www.ingramcontent.com/pod-product-compliance
Lightning Source LLC
Chambersburg PA
CBHW080539060326
40690CB00022B/5177